*"A handgun can be a very dangerous object.
But if you respect it, study it,
and learn to use it both well and wisely,
it may be the most important purchase
you will ever make."*

How to Shoot a Gun

is the essential handbook for every new gun owner.
Safe and effective gun handling starts with knowing
how to select, use, and maintain a firearm—the vital
information found in this indispensable guide.

*A gun can be your best defense.
Knowing how to use it safely is
your #1 protection.*

How to Shoot a Gun

JERRY PREISER

B

BERKLEY BOOKS, NEW YORK

This book is intended as a guide to the fundamental mechanics of firing a handgun. It is not intended as an advanced manual on firearms training.

Inexperienced gun owners should supplement the lessons learned from this book with supervised practice. A handgun is a deadly weapon. Some of the techniques described in this book, such as for loading or firing a gun, may, if misused, cause death or serious personal injury, for which the author and publisher disclaim any liability.

Unauthorized possession and use of a handgun or ammunition are criminal offenses in many jurisdictions.

HOW TO SHOOT A GUN

A Berkley Book / published by arrangement with
the author

PRINTING HISTORY
Berkley trade paperback edition / July 1984
Berkley mass market edition / July 1993

All rights reserved.
Copyright © 1984 by Jerry Preiser.
Interior photographs by Jeffrey Crespi.
Produced by Philip Lief & Associates / John Boswell Associates.
This book may not be reproduced in whole or in part,
by mimeograph or any other means, without permission.
For information address: The Berkley Publishing Group,
200 Madison Avenue, New York, New York 10016.

ISBN: 0-425-13844-5

A BERKLEY BOOK® TM 757,375
Berkley Books are published by The Berkley Publishing Group,
200 Madison Avenue, New York, New York 10016.
The name "BERKLEY" and the "B" logo
are trademarks belonging to Berkley Publishing Corporation.

PRINTED IN THE UNITED STATES OF AMERICA

10 9 8 7 6 5 4 3 2 1

CONTENTS

INTRODUCTION

The movies make it look so easy. If you ever have to use a firearm, you simply pull the trigger and *bang!*—you hit your target.

There's only one thing wrong with this image, and that's the fact that it simply doesn't happen that way in real life. A gun is not only a dangerous weapon when improperly used, it's a complicated piece of machinery that must be understood and maintained in order to be an asset and not a harmful hindrance.

Anyone who owns or is thinking of buying a gun needs this book. And this book is not all that is needed. What is needed, as you'll see in the chapters that follow, is practice, patience, and persistence.

In these pages you'll find the same basic information taught to every law enforcement officer. You'll learn which type of handgun is best suited for you and which kind of ammunition to purchase for that particular gun. You'll go through the steps of basic training and be instructed in defense maneuvers.

Equally important, you'll learn how to avoid accidents and how to keep your firearm in top condition. In short, when you finish reading this book, you'll be equipped with all the basic knowledge that any handgun owner must have. The rest—how diligently you practice, how much you familiarize yourself with your gun, how well you train yourself to use a weapon in an emergency—is up to you.

If you don't plan to practice and acquaint yourself with the techniques of marksmanship—if you plan to read this book and then stow it away in a drawer, next to your handgun—you are better off not owning a gun at all. If you don't know how to use a firearm properly, a gun in your hand is as dangerous as a gun that is being pointed at you by someone else.

Regular practice will pay off. You'll come to feel comfortable around guns and confident of your ability to fire a gun and hit your target. You will probably come to appreciate marksmanship as a sport in itself, to look forward to practice sessions, to feel a deeper sense of security when you are alone at home or in your car. A handgun can be a very dangerous object. But if you respect it, study it, and learn to use it both well and wisely, it may be the most important purchase you will ever make.

1

THE GUN

All handguns share three basic characteristics:

(1) They are portable.
(2) They are easy to store.
(3) They can be fired with either hand (or both hands).

Any gun that can be fired with either hand is properly known as a pistol, although this term is used today more in reference to the semiautomatics, which are usually called "automatics."

The word *pistol* comes from the town of Pistoia in northern Italy, where handguns were manufactured as early as the fifteenth and sixteenth centuries. The automatic is a far more recent invention, developed by John Browning at the end of the nineteenth century.

Handguns vary in shape, size, and weight, as well as in options available and type of ammunition used.

Any handgun can be divided into three major

The revolver is loaded by slipping a cartridge into the chamber, then rotating the cylinder to the next chamber.

parts: the barrel, the frame, and the action. A revolver's bullets are brought into line with the barrel and the hammer by the cylinder. Cartridges are held in the cylinder, which is usually located behind the barrel. Each time the revolver is cocked, the cylinder turns, bringing a fresh cartridge into position. There are two types of revolvers: single-action, in which the hammer must be manually pulled back to full cock before the trigger is pulled; and double-action, which can be fired by hand-cocking the hammer or by simply pulling the trigger. For defense purposes, only the double-action revolver will be considered.

The semiautomatic is also called a self-loader, and the main difference between it and a revolver is the

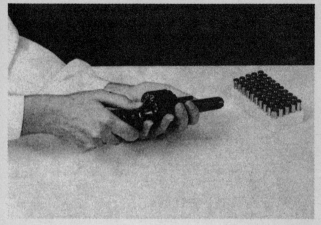

Action of the Smith & Wesson .38 revolver is easily opened and the cylinder lifted from the frame.

---

manner in which the cartridges are brought into firing position and ejected.

Cartridges are loaded into a magazine located in the grip of the gun. A spring at the bottom of the magazine forces the cartridges upward. At the top of the frame, the slide moves back and forth in firing, bringing a new cartridge into position each time; the slide contains the firing pin and extractor. Self-loaders are either single-action or double-action; however, unlike the single-action revolver, the single-action semiautomatic must be manually cocked just one time. Before the first shot, the slide must be pulled back manually, but after that, it automatically forces the next bullet up to the barrel.

Which type of gun is for you?

The ejector rod is used to push any spent cartridges from the cylinders of the revolver.

This will be taken up in Chapter Two, where you will learn that the type of gun you decide to purchase is mainly a matter of personal preference. To a large degree one handgun is much the same as another: Accuracy varies among both revolvers and self-loaders. However, one consideration is the safety factor.

Most handgun experts consider the revolver safer for the beginning shooter who plans to keep a gun in the car or the house. Since the revolver must be cocked before each shot is fired, and since it's easy to tell by a glance at the cylinder whether or not a bullet is in position to be fired, there is less chance of careless firing. With a semiautomatic the magazine must be removed or the safety applied to keep the gun from firing. Otherwise a fresh cartridge will always be ready to be positioned for firing.

Remember, regardless of what type of handgun you own, you should always **TREAT EVERY FIREARM AS IF IT WERE LOADED.** The handgun action should always be kept open and *unloaded* until ready to use.

LOADING THE REVOLVER

The typical revolver is easy to load.

First, place the revolver in the palm of your non-shooting hand with the barrel pointed down. With your right thumb, press the cylinder latch and use the middle two fingers of your left hand to swing the cylinder out of the frame.

The chambers are now exposed, and the left thumb can push the ejector rod to remove any empty cartridge cases, which can be caught in your free hand.

Keeping the muzzle pointed downward, slip fresh ammunition into the chambers, using the left thumb and two middle fingers to rotate the cylinder as each chamber is filled.

After loading, swing the cylinder back into the frame, making sure it's pushed all the way back. Never force the cylinder: Any resistance may be due to a high primer (particularly with reloads), and the bullet should be discarded.

ALWAYS KEEP YOUR FINGER OFF THE

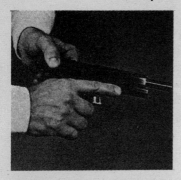

Action on the Colt .45 opened to remove any cartridge in the chamber.

The spring is pushed down and cartridges loaded into the magazine of the semiautomatic pistol.

TRIGGER AND THE MUZZLE POINTED DOWNWARD!

To unload, just swing the cylinder out and use the ejector rod as described above.

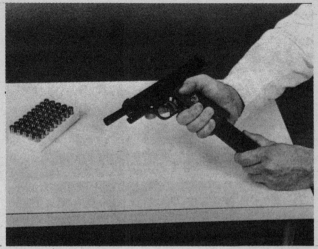

The .45 semiautomatic is easily loaded by slipping the magazine into the grip.

LOADING THE SEMIAUTOMATIC

To load the semiautomatic, you must first remove the magazine by pushing the magazine-release button.

After taking out the magazine, pull back on the slide to remove any cartridge from the chamber, then lock the slide open and double-check to make sure there is no cartridge left in the chamber.

To load the magazine, pull the follower plate down and stack cartridges on top of one another until the magazine is full.

When the magazine has been filled, insert it back into the grip and press the slide stop so that the slide will be released. As soon as the slide goes forward, a cartridge will be chambered and you'll be ready to fire.

If you don't wish to fire at this point, place the manual safety in the "on" position.

NOTE: Though some semiautomatics are equipped with a magazine connector that keeps the gun from firing when the magazine is removed, any mechanical part (disconnector or safety) can malfunction. **ALWAYS CHECK A SEMIAUTOMATIC TO MAKE CERTAIN THERE IS NO CARTRIDGE IN THE CHAMBER.** It is impossible to be overly cautious in this respect.

Now that you have a basic knowledge of handguns and how they work, you are ready to consider the purchase of a pistol for your personal use.

2

BUYING A GUN

Before you go out to purchase a handgun, you should first acquaint yourself with the laws regulating the purchase and transport of firearms in your state. In some states it is necessary to obtain a gun license even before buying the gun; in others a certain amount of time must elapse between the time you purchase a gun and the time it's delivered to you. Many states and local jurisdictions also have their own legislation.

Be sure to check your local laws regarding transportation of firearms before carrying your handgun anywhere (even away from the store where you've purchased it). Laws vary, some of them making it illegal to carry a gun that is loaded, one that is concealed (even in the glove compartment of an automobile), or one that is not in a case or a box.

In the United States, federal laws provide for reg-

19

istration through licensed dealers, so you should have acceptable identification on you when you set out to buy a firearm.

Who is *not* allowed to possess a firearm of any sort? According to federal law, you cannot own a gun or have one in your possession if:

(1) You have renounced your US citizenship.
(2) You've been dishonorably discharged from the military.
(3) You have been convicted of a felony.
(4) You are addicted to narcotics.
(5) You are under indictment.
(6) You've ever been treated for one of several types of mental illness.
(7) You are an illegal alien.

No matter where you live, you should register the serial number of your handgun with your local police department in case of theft.

Besides a gun, you will need ammunition, and you may wish to buy spare magazines or speed loaders as well. If you are planning to join a range, check with them to see if you'll need other accessories. Many ranges require members to supply their own protective devices for eyes and ears.

There are some rules for new handgun purchasers. First of all, no one who isn't planning regular practice should even consider a snub-nosed revolver—one with a barrel two inches long or shorter. Look for a gun with a barrel at least three inches long. Many experts recommend an official

A small-caliber semi-automatic, like this Smith & Wesson .22, is a good choice for target practice.

police revolver with a four-inch barrel and fixed sights.

Regardless of what model gun you wish to purchase, you'd be well advised to seek out one that has a match in a .22-caliber model. A beginner will be needing a lot of practice time at the range or out in the woods, and .22-caliber ammunition is the most economical. In addition, the .22 is an excellent training gun because it is lightweight and easy to handle, and has considerably less recoil than larger-caliber pistols.

When discussing semiautomatics, many experts are enthusiastic in their praise of the .45 ACP (Automatic Colt Pistol). The first-time handgun owner should realize that this self-loader is more difficult to master than the .38 revolver, and much more practice time should be allowed for if one is chosen. Also, the .45 ACP is a pistol that must be handled with special care. In some police departments these guns are loaded only when the muzzle is pointed downward into a deep barrel of sand.

The Colt .45 is one of the most popular and frequently purchased semi-automatics.

In choosing a gun, don't forget that, in general, the higher the caliber, the stronger the recoil. Body weight and strength must be taken into consideration, as well as where the gun will be kept.

It's wise to shop for a gun with an expert companion, someone who will be quick to spot any customizing or adaptations that may be undesirable in a defense weapon for a first-time owner.

In a defense gun, fixed sights are the most advisable. Adjustable sights, while a boon in competition, must be adjusted frequently. In a defensive situation one rarely has the time to check and adjust the sights.

Don't overlook the possibility of investing in a used handgun. Age doesn't detract from a firearm's adequacy or accuracy as long as the gun has been well maintained. In these cases a knowledgeable opinion is called for.

Personally, you should be concerned with the "feel" of the gun. Does it fit well in your hand? Is it neither too heavy nor too light? Does your finger fit the trigger well, and is it easy for you to fire? Can you see through the sights without difficulty? Does the heft

Secondhand revolvers are easily found: This is a .38 Smith & Wesson Model 10.

of the gun and its balance make it easy for you to raise it to shoot with accuracy?

If you have decided upon a used gun, never buy one without first firing it. You don't need to inherit someone else's problems with a malfunction or distortion in any of its mechanisms.

Choosing the proper handgun is a personal procedure. Your life may depend upon your choice one day, so it is not a selection to take lightly or one that you should make on an impulse.

If you are in a position where you must buy a used handgun without assistance, the following is a quick checklist of what to look for:

(1) Is the barrel securely anchored?
(2) Is the bore (the opening of the barrel) sharp and clean at the edges, indicating that it hasn't been too frequently used?
(3) Is the barrel smooth and unpitted when you glance through the bore?
(4) Is the firing pin on-center and the hole in the

breech-block through which it passes completely round? If not, it indicates that the gun will fire off-center.

(5) Is the trigger pull sharp, with no perceptible movement in the trigger itself?

(6) If a semiautomatic, is the slide in good repair and undamaged? Do all safety devices on the pistol function?

(7) If a revolver, does the cylinder rotate each chamber perfectly into line? Is the crane that supports the cylinder fitted tightly to the frame of the gun? When the gun is fully locked, attempt to rotate the cylinder in either direction, checking to make sure there's no excess play.

(8) Is the frame undistorted, with no warping? Is the muzzle undented?

(9) Are the screw heads sharp and clean (unburred), indicating that the gun has not been misused?

If possible, practice at a range that supplies guns for the shooters' use before investing in a handgun of your own. That way you'll have more of an idea what you're looking for in a gun before you look at the market. As with any commodity, buying a gun blindly is not a wise idea.

If you plan to purchase a new gun, you may wish to contact one of the major manufacturers to obtain a catalog. There is a list of these in the appendix at the back of this book.

The Second World War saw an influx of foreign firearms into the States. The most frequently encountered are the Luger, the Walther, and the Mauser (German); the Beretta (Italian); the Webley and the Enfield (British); and the Star, the Astra, and the Llama (Spanish). Many of these makes have American distributors and are sold in gun shops. Of course, numerous foreign service revolvers captured during combat are offered for sale in used condition. Before purchasing any gun— certainly before considering a foreign model—you should make certain that you can find a local gunsmith familiar with the firearm for any repairs or servicing.

Never purchase a gun unless you feel comfortable with it and trust it: That's the most important consideration of all.

3

AMMUNITION

The most important thing any gun owner must remember about ammunition is to know which ammunition can be fired with his or her gun. Just because a cartridge fits a particular chamber or magazine doesn't mean it's meant to be fired by that handgun, and attempting to fire the wrong ammunition can lead to serious accidents.

Beginners should fire *only* factory-manufactured cartridges or those from a recognized reloader. While experienced marksmen sometimes prepare their own cartridges, this is not for amateurs, and for safety's sake, only factory-made ammunition should be fired.

Cartridges are available in many different sizes, but there are only two types of ammunition: center-fire and rimfire.

The names refer to the location of the primer in the base of the cartridge. Rimfire ammunition has the primer located around the rim of the base, while

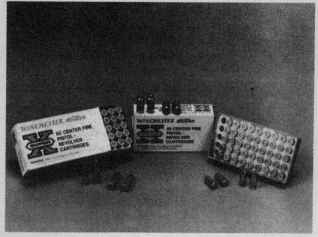

From left to right: .38, .45, and 9mm centerfire cartridges.

---

centerfire has the primer smack in the center.

The word *bullet* when referring to a complete cartridge is a misnomer. The bullet is only part of the cartridge, the part that is ejected from the barrel upon firing. The other components of the cartridge are the case, the primer, and the propellant, or powder.

The chemistry involved in firing a gun is quite simple. When the trigger is pulled, the hammer or firing pin is released by the firing mechanism and strikes the base of the cartridge, exploding the primer.

The detonation of the primer provides a spark, and it is this spark that ignites the powder. As the powder burns, gas is released and expands within the

Factory ammunition is packaged in well-marked boxes—in this case, for a .22 pistol.

cartridge case, thereby pushing the bullet out through the gun barrel with considerable force.

The creation of several thousand pounds of pressure per square inch by the burning powder takes only a fraction of a second. The bullets themselves are composed mostly or entirely of lead, and are very heavy in relation to their small size, which causes them to retain much of their original velocity when fired from a distance. This is important to remember when purchasing a gun and ammunition that may have to be used in heavily populated areas, as bullet weight has a great influence on how far a bullet can travel. Any bullet that may travel a great deal farther than intended is of danger to innocent bystanders.

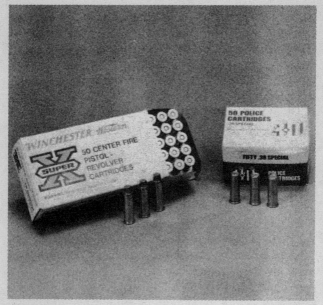

This .38 ammo shows the two types of bullets available: pointed and flat-nosed.

Ammunition is identified by the bullet's diameter in inches or millimeters, with a certain amount of leeway for imprecision. In other words a .357 Magnum cartridge is a case containing a bullet that is .357 inches in diameter. (A .38 Special bullet is the same diameter, which shows that, while not always exact, the caliber will always be very close to the bullet's actual diameter.) A 9mm cartridge's bullet is nine millimeters in diameter.

Until the new gun owner has become familiar with various cartridges, the advice of an expert or gun shop owner should be relied upon when purchasing ammunition. The ammunition box should be labeled and each cartridge case should be stamped to identify the ammunition.

There are many considerations regarding which type bullet is best for which type of shooting. For self-defense situations the soft- or hollow-point bullet is the wisest purchase, as these bullets expand upon impact more than other types of ammunition, making them less likely to ricochet or travel too far out of target range.

Lead bullets are more effective than steel- and copper-jacketed bullets of the same weight. Flat-nosed bullets are more destructive than pointed ones. Semiautomatics and revolvers fire different ammunition.

Regardless of what type of gun and ammunition you purchase, for safety's sake, ammunition should be stored in a separate place.

If you plan to practice at a range, check to see if they supply the ammunition. If they do, they usually charge by the round. A round of ammunition does not refer, as some nonshooters think, to a complete cylinder or magazine of ammunition; it is simply one complete cartridge, ready for firing.

4

STARTING TO SHOOT

Now that you've got a gun, you can begin practicing some of the fundamentals important to good shooting before you even head for your local practice range. The more you familiarize yourself with these basics, the easier you'll find marksmanship training and the shorter your training period will be. Unless you become a full member of a practice range (and sometimes even then), you'll be charged for practice time there, so pre-range sessions at home will also represent a financial savings.

ALL PRE-RANGE PRACTICE SHOULD BE PERFORMED WITH AN UNLOADED GUN! You are not going to shoot now. You are simply preparing yourself for your initial shooting sessions.

THE GRIP

A gun is never simply picked up in the shooting hand. First, hold the gun in your nonshooting hand, cradling it just under the trigger guard. If the gun is

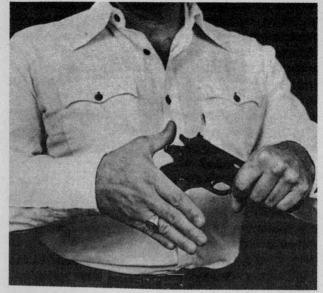

Always use your nonshooting hand to place the gun, muzzle down, into the V of your shooting hand.

a revolver, use the thumb of your shooting hand to pull the hammer back to the full-cock position. Then place the thumb of your nonshooting hand between the hammer and the frame to prevent accidental firing.

Place the gun in your shooting hand, leaving your nonshooting hand where it is. The V formed by the thumb and index finger of your shooting hand should be as high as possible on the grip without interfering with the movement of the hammer (revolver) or slide (semiautomatic pistol). With a semiautomatic, make certain the webbing between the thumb and trigger finger of your shooting hand is below the slide to avoid cutting yourself.

The thumb of your nonshooting hand should stay between the hammer and the frame of a revolver until the gun is extended for firing. The thumb of the shooting hand should rest along the frame on top of the cylinder latch. If you're firing a semiautomatic, the thumb of the shooting hand should rest horizontally along the frame, below the slide. **NEVER REST YOUR THUMB WHERE IT WILL INTERFERE WITH YOUR TRIGGER FINGER.**

Your index finger should be placed on the trigger where it is comfortable and at the same time able to exert enough pressure to squeeze off a shot. In most cases this will be almost up to the first joint or with the pad of the first joint against the trigger.

The nonshooting hand is used to give additional support in the two-handed grip by holding the pistol and the shooting hand. **DO NOT PLACE YOUR HAND OR FINGERS IN FRONT OF THE MUZZLE OF ANY GUN OR ALONGSIDE THE GAP BETWEEN THE BARREL AND CYLINDER OF A REVOLVER.** Hot gases, as well as small particles of lead, escape at these spots upon firing and can cause injury if an improper grip is used.

The other three fingers of your shooting hand should be curled around the grip, holding it firmly

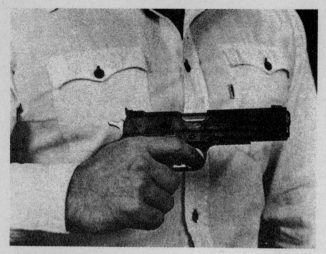

Hold the semiautomatic so no part of the shooting hand interferes with the action of the slide.

enough for control but not so tightly that muscle tremors result and throw off firing accuracy.

Practice picking up and gripping the gun until it becomes second nature to you and you feel comfortable with it in your hand. Concentrate on assuming the same grip each time you put the gun in your hand.

THE STANCE

It is recommended that beginners use the two-handed grip for better control. If a one-handed grip

The Weaver stance: Trigger finger is kept off the trigger until arms are extended for firing.

is used, be sure your nonshooting hand rests where it is immobilized, because if it swings free, it will affect your aim. The best place for the nonshooting hand in a one-handed grip is on the hip or in the pocket.

At the range itself you may be encouraged to start off in a bench-supported position. This simply means sitting down behind the bench, with the pistol gripped in your hands and your hands resting on a sandbag on top of the bench. This position aids

One-handed target-shooting stance: Shooting arm is straight, while nonshooting hand is immobilized.

In any shooting stance, feet should be shoulder width apart, pointed slightly outward.

in eliminating unnecessary movement while the new shooter is mastering the fundamentals of marksmanship.

In a standing position, feet should be spread about shoulder width apart, with toes pointed slightly outward for even weight distribution and balance.

The stance favored for speed and accuracy in defensive situations is the Weaver stance, named after marksman Jack Weaver, who developed it in 1958.

For the right-handed shooter, the Weaver stance is assumed as follows (if shooting with the left hand, simply reverse directions):

(1) Holding your body erect, stand with your left foot leading slightly, your left shoulder leading as well, and knees straight. You should be facing the target almost squarely.

(2) Your head should be erect or bent slightly into the sight line. With the pistol raised so you can aim through the sights, your right hand should grip the gun as high as possible, while the left hand wraps horizontally over the right. The thumb of the left hand should be over the right hand when firing a semiautomatic or crossed over when shooting a revolver. The pistol will then be supported as it rests on the middle of the second joint of your left index finger.

(3) The shooting arm should be straight or slightly flexed, at no more than a 10-degree

The Weaver stance: Nonshooting hand supports shooting hand and gun.

angle, while the left arm is bent at an angle of 30 to 45 degrees.

You should practice your stance as you practiced your grip, so that you can assume it at a moment's notice without worrying whether your feet are positioned correctly or your elbows are bent enough. Now you are ready to work on the one other element of marksmanship you can practice before shooting at the range. This is getting used to aiming by proper use of the gun's sights.

The Weaver stance: Elbow of nonshooting arm is slightly bent, back is straight.

THE SIGHTS

Almost any gun you will be picking up these days will make use of the Partridge sight, named after E. E. Partridge, the man who invented it in the last century. The Partridge sight consists of a front sight and a rear sight; the front sight is simply a vertical iron post, flat on top and with vertical sides. The rear sight is a rectangular piece with a square notch in it. To take aim, the front sight is positioned to fill the rear sight. The top of the front post should

The Weaver stance: When properly assumed, this stance allows shooter to face target almost squarely.

The correct combat grip: Nonshooting hand provides support without interfering with the shooting hand.

be flush with the top of the rear notch, and the front post should almost fill the space of the rear notch, with just a thin ribbon of light on either side. (These ribbons of light should be exactly the same width.)

What happens if you squeeze off a shot when the sights are not properly aligned? There are four possibilities:

(1) If the front sight is off-center and closer to the left side of the rear sight, the shot will hit too far to the left.

Good "six-o'clock hold" but impossible sighting: The human eye cannot focus clearly on both sights and target at once.

The shooter learns from his targets: Here the grouping is good but shots went too low and too far to the right.

(2) If the front sight is off-center and closer to the right side of the rear sight, the shot will hit too far to the right.

(3) If the front sight is higher than the rear sight (i.e., instead of being flush with the top of the rear notch, the front post's flat top rises above it), the shot will go high.

(4) If the front sight dips between the sides of the rear notch, the shot will go low.

It is necessary for the sights to be in a fixed position—the proper position—each and every time a

Good sighting: The sights are in sharp focus at the six-o'clock hold, while the bull's-eye is slightly blurred.

gun is fired. It is for this reason that beginners (or anyone who plans to fire a gun irregularly and not on a competition basis) are advised to purchase a gun with *fixed* sights. Fixed sights cannot be adjusted, except by a competent gunsmith. By the same token fixed sights will not slip but will remain accurate.

The "sight picture" is the term given to what you see when your aligned sights are on the target. If possible, you should keep both eyes open when aiming. This gives you more light and better depth perception, while your stronger eye will still control your aim.

The proper sight picture when aiming is known as the "six-o'clock hold," and most guns are factory-aligned for this. This means that when you're aiming at a bull's-eye, the aiming point will be the bottom of the bull, or the six-o'clock position on an imaginary clock face. Some shooters prefer to set their sights for a center hold—to aim smack at the center of the bull's eye—but six o'clock is recommended for beginners.

This, then, is the difference between sight alignment and sight picture: *Sight alignment* refers to the proper alignment of the front sight in the middle of the rear sight, while *sight picture* refers to the correct placement of the target within those sights. In the case of the six-o'clock hold, this means the bull's-eye should appear to rest directly atop the front sight as it fills the rear sight, its flat top flush with the tops of both sides of the rear notch and with a thin ribbon of light on either side of the front sight. (These ribbons of light should be of equal width.)

You take aim by looking at the target *through* the sights, not *at* the sights. You should be able to see the sights clearly and the bull's-eye slightly out of focus.

DRY FIRING

No shooter should ever cease to practice dry firing: Many pros recommend dry firing fifty "shots" a day to keep in shape. The importance of dry firing (*dry firing* means going through all the motions of firing with an unloaded gun) cannot be stressed enough for the beginner. When dry firing, a good tip is to use a spent cartridge to protect the firing mechanism.

Why is dry firing so vital? Simply consider the mechanics involved in shooting a gun for a moment. The average handgun weighs 2½ pounds. When you pull the trigger, you must exert a certain amount of pressure, which is called the trigger pull. On a .22 automatic, the trigger pull runs from about 2¾ pounds to 3 pounds, while on a .38 revolver it runs 3 to 3½ pounds.

It doesn't take a physics expert to realize that the application of 3 pounds of pressure is going to set up sizable tremors in a 2½-pound object. It takes practice to be able to exert enough pressure on the trigger without ending up with a jerky movement. Many shooters practice building up the muscles in their shooting arm even when not holding a gun. This can be done with a rubber ball and a repetitive squeeze/relax cycle.

Dry firing is also important in helping the beginner learn to control flinching. The novice shooter usually flinches automatically from the anticipation of the noise and the recoil, neither of which are present, of course, with an empty gun. **NEVER BEGIN DRY FIRING WITHOUT FIRST CHECKING TO MAKE SURE THE GUN IS UNLOADED!** Even if you just bought the gun and are certain there is no bullet in the chamber, check. Don't forget the first rule of shooting: **ALWAYS TREAT A GUN AS IF IT'S LOADED.**

5

INTRODUCTION TO MARKSMANSHIP

Any beginner should practice, if at all possible, at a range run by professionals. The main reasons for this are obvious. The convenience of a range allows the new shooter to practice regardless of the time and the weather, and without having to find a spot where the noise will not disrupt the peace. The safety factor makes the range an ideal place as well.

In addition, the presence of a qualified professional is strongly advised to keep the new shooter from picking up bad habits. Once acquired, bad shooting habits aren't easy to unlearn, and being taught by an expert will keep you from acquiring them in the first place. Only practice makes perfect, and the value of that practice is multiplied when a professional is present to explain exactly what was done improperly and how shooting can be improved.

You have already become somewhat familiar with

the four major elements of marksmanship in your own home. These are trigger control, stance, sight alignment, and gun-and-hand contact (or grip).

One other factor of prime importance that is sometimes not taken into consideration by the beginner (especially one who lacks proper coaching) is breathing. The arm and hand of the handgun shooter constitute the gun platform. Without proper breath control, this platform will waver and wobble, and there is no chance of accuracy.

Both the breath and the heartbeat influence the approach to a shot. Calmness is an important factor in the regulation of both. It's only natural for the beginner to be nervous and excited when learning to shoot, just as it's only natural that a surge of emotion will be overpoweringly present if you should be called upon to use your gun in a defensive situation. **RIGHT NOW IS THE TIME TO LEARN TO SEPARATE YOUR EMOTIONS FROM YOUR SKILLS WHEN FIRING.**

This means getting used to target practice at rapid speeds, in order to function efficiently and coolly under pressure. It also means gaining control over your breathing, so you will breathe properly *automatically* each time you raise your gun to fire it. Proper breathing is a habit, and only practice will enable a habit to become ingrained.

You don't need a gun in your hand to see how breathing affects your aim. Stand with your shooting arm stretched out in front of you. Now inhale keeping your eyes on your hand. Do you see how your hand rises? As your lungs expand, your chest lifts, and as your chest rises, so does your arm.

Now exhale and watch your arm drop slightly as you do so. Normal breathing while shooting will set the shooting arm moving in a seesaw motion. No matter how slight the motion of your arm when you breathe, it is enough to destroy your aim.

The only way to guarantee accuracy is to hold your breath. Since a shot will ordinarily be fired within a matter of seconds, the experienced marksman need not worry about oxygen starvation, which begins about fifteen seconds after taking a breath and holding it. The beginner, tense and hesitant, should realize that the first sign of oxygen starvation is difficulty keeping the target in focus, which progresses to an actual blurring of eyesight. Should you begin having difficulty focusing on the target when you first start shooting, stop and take a deep breath. With your finger off the trigger, lower the gun to a rest position and relax your grip until you have recovered.

The normal breathing sequence should be as follows: Take a normal breath, let it out while bringing your gun to position, then hold it while aiming and shooting. Keep your gun raised for the follow-through, then lower it and relax.

You will also work on trigger control at the range. It is important that the trigger finger move independently when exerting pressure on the trigger. Your grip should remain constant, with the gripping fingers and the thumb remaining immobile. At the same time, while squeezing off your shot, your concentration must not waver from the target: You should be focused on the front sight, which has been

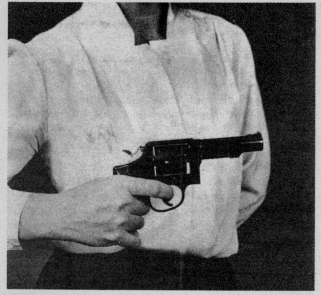

The proper grip on a revolver is firm but relaxed, allowing for controlled movement of the trigger finger.

---

correctly aligned with the rear sight and trained on the target at the six-o'clock hold.

Squeezing off your shot isn't simply a matter of "pulling" the trigger. First, you must take up any free movement, or slack, in the trigger. Next, initial pressure is applied, a light pressure that's approximately one quarter or less of the total pressure required to fire the gun.

The shot is controlled by increasing the pressure on the trigger smoothly and gradually—but not

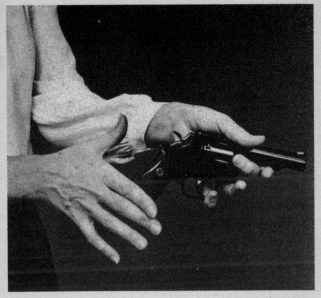

The V approach: The .38 revolver is placed into the shooting hand with the nonshooting hand.

slowly—applying what is called "positive" pressure. The entire shot should be released in two to five seconds. You should strive for a "surprise" break of the shot, with no anticipation.

Your grip greatly influences trigger control, and this is one reason why it's important that you grip your pistol correctly and that you're able to grip it in the same manner each and every time. Your trigger finger on its own must exert approximately three pounds of pressure on the trigger, and a stable, well-supported grip is necessary to keep your gun from wavering during the process.

The most serious and common error made by the beginner is jerking—applying a too-abrupt pressure on the trigger, which is accompanied by movement of the hand and arm muscles.

Jerking can be caused by several different factors, including blinking, flinching, and rushing through the shot. The usual result of jerking is shots too far to the left and down. The cure for jerking is to practice at the range with only one or two live rounds and the rest empties. Without looking at the cylinder, close it and begin firing. This will reveal any errors. With a semiautomatic, the coach/pupil method (in which your coach hands you the pistol without telling you if it's loaded) should be used.

Another common error is "holding too long," or drawing out the action of pressing the trigger. This is not unusual in a beginner who fears making a bad shot and is overcautious as a result. The shooter may hold his or her breath so long that the sight picture wavers and it's impossible to take proper aim, or the shooter may let one favorable moment after another go past until the chance for a good shot is gone. Then again, the shooter simply may not exert enough steady pressure on the trigger to release the shot.

It's difficult for the neophyte to squeeze gradually *and* quickly at the same time, and it's not unusual to go to one extreme or the other: Squeezing too gradually results in holding too long, while squeezing too quickly results in jerking. Good trigger control can be acquired only through practice, and this is an area in which plenty of dry-firing practice as well as shooting live rounds at the range will really pay off.

Once your range instructor is confident that you understand the fundamentals of shooting—the grip, stance, loading and unloading, breathing, trigger control, and so on—he will commence your program of basic training. It cannot be stressed enough how practice pays off, and your practice in shooting under various conditions will develop confidence and skills.

6
BASIC TRAINING

Most basic training consists of slow fire, timed fire, and rapid fire, as well as learning to obey range commands. Slow fire is especially important to the new shooter, as it allows plenty of time for concentration and rest between shots. During slow fire, ten minutes are allowed in which to get off ten shots. This gives you a full minute per shot, plenty of time in which to think about what you're doing and what you did in the last shot, along with its results.

Before commencing to fire, you should always make sure your feet are correctly positioned in relation to the target. Do this by setting your feet so you think they're in the best position. Then close your eyes and, keeping them closed, raise your gun and try to put your sights on where you think the target is. Without moving, open your eyes and check to see how far off you are. Keep your hand where it is while readjusting your feet to bring your sights in line with the target. Return your hand to resting po-

Ear and eye protectors are a requirement at most shooting ranges.

sition, then close your eyes again and repeat the procedure. When your hand is automatically lined up, you've found your best position.

There is a suggested shot sequence for each type of firing. The recommended sequence for slow fire is as follows:

(1) Extend your arm and breathe normally.
(2) Settle into a minimum arc of arm movement.
(3) Align your sights in the aiming area.
(4) Take up your trigger slack and apply initial pressure.
(5) Hold your breath.
(6) Concentrate on maintaining sight alignment as well as minimal movement.

(7) Start applying positive trigger pressure, keeping it steady, striving for the "surprise" break of the shot, with no anticipation.

(8) Concentrate your focus on the front sight.

(9) Fire and follow through.

Lower your gun to the resting position between shots and relax until your breathing returns to normal.

Timed fire and rapid fire are much the same, the only difference being the length of time allowed. Timed fire allows twenty seconds for each five-shot string, while rapid fire allows only ten seconds for the same string of shots.

In timed and rapid fire, you raise your gun at the command "Ready on the right," which is when you align your sights and begin your initial pressure on the trigger. At the command "Ready on the firing line" you will begin holding your breath.

The following is the sequence for timed and rapid fire, along with the commands you'll be given on the range:

(1) The range officer announces either rapid fire or timed fire, "with five rounds load." At this point you'll load and assume your proper grip. Breathe rhythmically and normally as he asks, "Is the line ready?" Check the position of your target.

(2) The range officer's command "Ready on the right" is your signal to extend the shooting arm with a stiff wrist and a locked elbow

and to align your sights. Breathe deeply and exhale while doing so.

(3) When the range officer commands "Ready on the left," find the aiming area at the edge of the target frame while you take your final deep breath and settle into a minimum arc of movement.

(4) As soon as you hear "Ready on the firing line," partly release your breath, then hold it. Focus on the front sight, take up your slack, and apply your initial pressure. As soon as the target faces toward you, begin your positive trigger pressure and concentrate on your sight alignment. Fire, maintaining focus for the follow-through.

After the first shot you have time for only a quick recovery while you maintain an approximate alignment of your sights. Your gun should remain pointed in the center of the aiming area and you must already be reapplying positive trigger pressure as you correct your sight alignment for the next shot. Rhythm is important in timed and rapid fire, and only by sticking to the proper shooting sequence can you develop the good rhythm you're seeking.

"Calling the shot" is another element of vital importance in both slow and rapid fire. Although the shooter won't know exactly *when* the gun will fire, a mental picture of the sight alignment in relation to the bull's-eye will tell the shooter where the bullet should hit. Failure to hit where the shooter expected indicates flinching, jerking, or something else that needs correction.

Needless to say, practice loses much of its worth if the shooter doesn't make a careful analysis of each session. This is where a professional's opinion comes in very handy, as the beginner often can't figure out why the shot didn't hit as called.

In slow fire, a bad shot requires that you ask yourself these questions:

(1) Did I correctly establish my minimum arc of movement?

(2) Did I keep my concentration on my sight alignment and not let it drift to my trigger control?

(3) Did I maintain point focus on my sight alignment?

(4) Was my trigger pressure steady and smooth? Or was it intermittent, with considerable effort needed to fire the gun?

(5) Did I follow my shooting sequence?

(6) Did I hold too long?

In any series of shots, check to see if there is an error pattern indicating that the same mistake was made on each shot. Don't forget to take into consideration your basics as well as your shooting sequence. Did you maintain a proper grip and a correct stance? Was your breathing controlled? Was your elbow locked against shifting movement? Did you flinch from the recoil or cringe from the noise of the shot?

In a string of timed or rapid fire, you will be checking for pretty much the same things, as well as asking yourself the following:

(1) Did I fire the first shot on time?
(2) Did I maintain rhythm through the sequence?
(3) Did I check for minor errors in my hold so that these could be corrected before the next shot was fired?

Most ranges provide the shooter with a work sheet on which to keep track of errors and the steps taken to correct them. In this way a shooter can keep track of progress and always be aware of the mistakes of the last session before beginning the next one.

Most shooters must pay special attention to recoil anticipation, as in most cases this is sheer reflex action, but nevertheless an action that keeps the shot from hitting the target.

The startle reflex generally takes three forms. Jerking, as we said earlier, is the result of the shooter rushing in an attempt to beat his or her own reflexes. By putting an extra squeeze into the shot, the shooter pushes the sight picture to the left, and the shot hits the seven-o'clock area.

Heeling occurs when the shooter attempts to absorb the recoil of the gun before it's even fired, pushing with the heel of the hand at the point of firing. This will send the shots into the one-o'clock position on the target.

Eye blink is yet another reflex made in preparation for being startled. Think of how we tend to blink before someone pulls a party cracker or when a firecracker is lit. Eye blink can throw the shot off in any direction.

The answer to correcting any shooter errors is, of

course, practice and more practice. Dry firing should be practiced daily if possible, only for ten minutes or so at first, then building up to half an hour as the arm becomes conditioned. Still, there's no substitute for live firing: Only a loaded gun will show you exactly where you slipped up when firing at the target.

Shooting on a practice range is shooting under *optimal* conditions. Only when you have total confidence in your ability on the range and have managed to clean up any errors in your shooting can you hope to perform well under less-than-ideal conditions. And very few, if any, defensive situations are perfect.

7

DEFENSE TRAINING

Anyone who joins a range or gun club or who signs up for a self-defense firearms course will be taught all the fundamentals of shooting and will be expected to master both slow-fire and rapid-fire techniques. For those who have purchased a gun for defense purposes, quite a few ranges and courses offer special defense-tactics training. This is especially true of those that have outdoor facilities.

Naturally, should the awful time arrive when your life is threatened, your attacker won't be standing in bright light like a sitting duck. Nor will he remain still or simply sway from side to side until he's picked off. This is where special defense training and techniques come in.

Prone techniques are taught, as well as barricade techniques that can be adapted to the home front— shooting from the cover of a bed or doorway or from around the corner of a house. Night shooting will be covered as well (this is one time when customized

Defense shooting: At the ready, nonshooting hand is already in support position.

colored sights come in handy, because it's difficult to focus on regular sights in the dark).

In addition to these areas, you'll have advanced study in aiming at moving targets and so-called "instinct" shooting. Defense courses today—except in police training—don't focus on holstering and quick-draw techniques. Few people who buy a gun for their own safety plan to be "packing" it, and most quick-draw techniques are saved for competitions. Should you want to learn the various draws, learn them through professional instruction: More than one novice handgunner has taken a bullet in the foot or finger when trying to show off with clumsy fast-draw techniques. Under no circumstances should you attempt any fancy cross-draws. Drawing a firearm

Defensive shooting skills require continued practice.

across your own body is asking for trouble; besides, there's no reason you'll ever need to do it.

One important consideration that some shooters overlook is mastering loading and reloading in the dark. You won't always be in a situation where you can flick on the light and casually load your gun, so

you should be as familiar with your weapon with
your eyes closed as with your eyes open. This is a
time for remembering handgun safety. Shooters are
more likely to forget to keep the muzzles of their
guns pointed downward in darkness; remember, just
because you can't see what you're doing doesn't make
it *safer*. Extra caution is called for.

Depending on how comprehensive your study of
self-defense is, you'll learn where to aim and how to
place your shots, how to identify someone else's gun
by the sound and/or shape of it, and various defense
postures, such as hip-supported shooting.

No one should own a gun without knowing the ca-
pabilities of that particular firearm. In a life-or-
death situation you can't afford to waste ammunition
by squeezing off useless shots. Every weapon and
type of ammunition has a certain range and man-
stopping potential. You should familiarize yourself
with all the facts and figures available on the gun
you'll be using. It's also a good idea to know as much
as possible about other commonly used handguns.

Much emphasis is placed on instinct and mental
conditioning in defense training. Being able to hit
the target every time at the range isn't going to help
when you're under attack unless you can function in
a dangerous situation. Even some police officers are
stunned to discover how much of their training they
forget or how paralyzed they become when the target
is human.

Many courses integrate a study of the legality of
armed defense in their lessons. Just because an in-
truder has entered your house doesn't mean you're
legally in the right to pull out a gun and shoot, and

nobody should possess a firearm without knowing the legal ramifications of his actions.

No good defense trainer will encourage you to shoot unless you have to. Just as a gun can save your life, so are you gambling unnecessarily with your life if you cock that pistol without due cause.

Defense training should be considered only after you have mastered the basic skills of shooting. It makes no difference how many shooting techniques you're familiar with or whether you can reload your gun in the dark if you haven't a prayer of hitting your target.

Even after your training is completed, you should continue to practice regularly. For defensive purposes nothing is more important than keeping your skills honed and never letting them grow rusty. To this end, the most important exercises to be practiced remain the most basic. As long as you have a gun in your possession, you should continue with a regular schedule of dry firing and slow firing. Buying a gun, learning how to use it, and then stashing it away in a drawer and forgetting about it never did anyone a bit of good in an emergency.

8

PREPARING AND PERSONALIZING A GUN

To the beginner, customized firearms may sound like something only cowboys, collectors, and match competitors would be interested in. This isn't the case at all.

A handgun is manufactured with a grip, trigger, sights, hammer, and so forth designed to fit someone who doesn't exist in reality: the average man. If you carry a gun for defensive purposes, you want that gun to be its most effective. In many cases this means adapting your gun to your personal needs, and it requires the assistance of a customizer.

The grip adapter or custom grip will give you a gun that fits your hand perfectly. Depending on the size of your hand, you may need a smaller or larger grip than was on the gun to begin with.

Trigger shoes are called for if your trigger finger is too long for the trigger. Unless you have a trigger

The speed loader is used at many ranges to facilitate rapid reloading of the revolver. Note typical grip adapter used to enlarge grip.

shoe fitted to your gun, your finger will rest on the trigger incorrectly.

If you encounter difficulty cocking the hammer of your gun, you may want to look into having a hammer adapter or shoe put on.

Customized sights are a boon to any shooter, especially the beginner, who often has difficulty focusing on the sights in the first place. On a gun that will be used for defensive purposes, customized sights can be a matter of life or death. As we already stated, shooting at a range means shooting under controlled conditions. Shooting defensively can mean shooting in the dark or shooting outdoors in bad weather. A gold block or red plastic insert set into the front sight improves sight alignment tremendously. Almost any custom sight will be much easier to focus with than a factory sight.

Safeties can also be customized; magazines can be adapted for faster reloading.

One customizing job that is useless as well as dangerous in most instances is customizing the trigger pull to hair-trigger proportions. If your trigger doesn't pull easily, you will be better off having the action honed so that it will fire faster. Added practice should let any shooter gain control over the trigger pull without adaptations.

Some of the adaptations and customizing used by police officers and professional marksmen is superfluous and ill-advised for a nonprofessional. You don't need a concealment butt or a shortened barrel.

For the first-time gun buyer, then, the only adaptations he should consider are grip adapter, trigger shoe, hammer adapter, and customized sights. Fixed sights are suggested over adjustable sights; this is an uncomplicated procedure that any competent gunsmith can perform.

Like the neophyte skier who can't resist buying everything in the sports shop, the new gun owner often ends up with a mass of equipment and accessories that will never be used. The best advice is to purchase whatever will be needed at your practice range to begin with—and nothing more. The gun shops will still be there in two or three weeks, and if you decide you really want a bunch of fancy accessories, you can buy them at that time, when you'll at least know what they're for and if you'll make use of them.

The Browning 9mm pistol was named after the inventor of the semiautomatic.

When buying a holster, keep in mind that you're not planning to become the local fast-draw champion. Any holster you purchase should be chosen on the basis of how well it protects the gun. Cartridge carriers and ammunition pouches are useful for the same reason: They will protect your ammunition and make storage easier. Speed-loaders and spare magazines are a necessity for competitions and sometimes required at practice ranges, but these are not necessary for anyone purchasing a gun for self-defense, since in such situations you shouldn't need more than six cartridges in your pistol.

You'll have no call for any ammunition other than factory cartridges. The beginner does best by sticking to basics and can be advised by a range officer on how to do this. It's not wise to rely on just any gun dealer when purchasing accessories or on any gunsmith when deciding upon customizing. Remember, these men are still salesmen, and it may be to their advantage to talk the customer into spending as much as possible. Ask your local range to recommend a reputable dealer.

Spend your money for maintenance instead. You must be willing to devote time and effort to keeping your gun clean and in proper upkeep, and you'll be less likely to regret cash paid out for the proper cleaning materials than you will for an expensive hand-carved mahogany grip, which is good for nothing but decorative purposes.

9
MAINTENANCE

Allowing dirt and grease to build up in your handgun is tantamount to issuing an open invitation: "Trouble, come on in!" If you think you'll be too busy or too indifferent to keep your gun in tip-top shape, you are better off not purchasing a gun at all. On the other hand, if you maintain its upkeep, a firearm will last a lifetime.

First of all, you should pick one place—a bench or table—where you can work on your gun all the time. You should keep all your cleaning supplies at this location. A good place to keep your cloths, patches, brushes, and solutions is in a big plastic fishing-tackle box. These are sold cheaply at most big discount stores.

You'll need some soft, untreated cotton cloths; one expert swears by cotton diapers, which can be washed in a machine and will last a long time. You'll also need patches.

There are two kinds of patches—cotton ones and

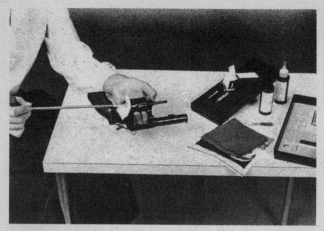

Revolver chambers are cleaned by attaching a saturated patch to the point of the ramrod and sliding it through the chamber.

the newer ones made of an abrasive mesh material. Patches are used for cleaning the outside of the gun as well as the chamber and barrel. These patches come in various sizes, and you'll need the proper size to cover the ramrod tip you'll be using. The patch must fit snugly into the chambers and the bore when wrapped around the ramrod. The ramrods that are easiest to use are stainless steel, with a sharp point on the end to hold the patch in place. You'll also need a wire brush, a cleaning solvent, an anti-rust treatment, and gun oil. You should also keep some chemical tightener on hand, a boon for loose screws and grips.

The revolver and the semiautomatic are cleaned

differently, and it's best to deal with them as separate subjects.

CLEANING THE REVOLVER

(1) **UNLOAD THE REVOLVER, THEN CHECK AND RECHECK TO MAKE SURE IT IS EMPTY.** Leaving the cylinder open, lay it down on the bench or table on top of the cleaning cloth.

(2) With a patch saturated with solvent, wipe the whole exterior of the gun. Clean the front and rear of the cylinder, all around the extractor head, and every part of the frame, then wipe off with a dry cloth.

(3) Fit another saturated patch to the end of the ramrod and pass it through the barrel. Use fresh patches for the cylinder chambers. After you've applied the solvent to the barrel and chambers, run your wire brush through them, being careful to run the brush in one direction only, as rubbing it back and forth can scratch the barrel.

(4) After cleaning with the brush, use the ramrod and a freshly saturated patch on these parts again, repeating until the patch emerges quite clean. Don't get carried away, though: Excessive cleaning can wear out a gun.

(5) Now put a clean, *dry* patch on the ramrod and run it through the barrel and chambers. Place a patch on the recoil plate and look

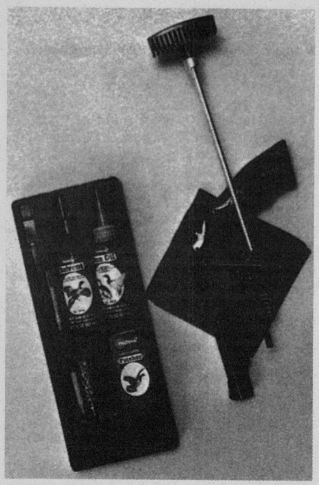

Typical cleaning supplies: The ramrod is being used to clean the cylinders of a Smith & Wesson .38 revolver.

down the barrel through the muzzle to make sure it's clean. If it's not, reclean.

(6) With a screwdriver, check all screws for tightness; put tightener on any screws that are repeatedly loosened (a drop of clear nail polish under the heads of screws that work loose will remedy the situation).

(7) After the gun is cleaned and dried, you may want to oil the moving parts. A single drop in the cylinder hand, at the hammer base, and into the cylinder-locking lug recess in the bottom of the frame will do. After oiling, close the cylinder and work the mechanism a few times before wiping off excess oil.

(8) If you'll be storing the revolver after cleaning it, or using it in any adverse weather conditions, it's not a bad idea to add a light coating of a preservative oil spray to the exterior of the gun; always do this with the cylinder closed.

CLEANING THE PISTOL

(1) **MAKE SURE THE PISTOL IS UN-LOADED: MAGAZINE OUT AND CHAMBER EMPTY.** Wipe it off with a clean gun cloth, then strip it and lay out the component parts.

(2) Saturate a patch with solvent and clean the receiver, the ramp, the slide rails, and the inside of the magazine.

Here the Colt .45 is in the "safe" position, with the action open and magazine removed.

(3) Drop the hammer and check the base to see that it's clean and free of residue, then cock the hammer and check the rest of the base. Wipe and clean everything forward of the feeding ramp. Make sure you remove any lubricant or gas residue left behind by the slide.

(4) Remove the barrel and clean it with a patch and ramrod inside and a solvent-soaked patch outside. You need not strip the slide for cleaning each and every time, but keep track of when you've cleaned its components so that it will be gone over every four times. Wipe everything clean with dry patches.

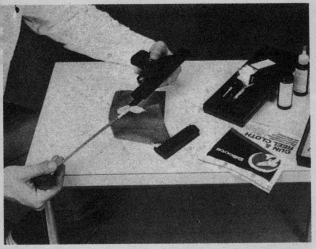

When cleaning the bore, slide the ramrod and patch through in one direction only, to prevent scratching.

(5) Run a clean, dry patch through the barrel before reassembling the pistol. Make sure no trace of solvent remains.

(6) Dry all the components and reassemble the pistol; then, as with the revolver, check screws and spray the exterior of the gun with preservative oil. Wipe off the excess and store the gun in its holster.

Never allow excess oil to remain on a revolver or semiautomatic. Wipe it off so there's never more than a light film of oil on the gun. Also, keep all your

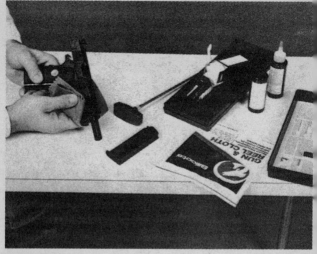

The exterior of the handgun should be cleaned with as much care as the chambers and bore.

ammunition clean. It takes just a single grain of sand or dirt to scratch the bore of the gun.

Even if you store your gun and aren't using it, it should be cleaned at least twice a year—more if it's somewhere where it's affected by weather, salt air, or humidity.

If, as you're cleaning your firearm, you spot repairs that should be made, don't attempt to do them yourself. Other than tightening screws, all repairs, no matter how minor, should be performed by the manufacturer or a reliable gunsmith.

Remember, the most important thing about cleaning your gun is simply to do it—each and every time it's fired.

10

FIREARMS SAFETY

Properly handled and respected, a gun is no more dangerous than any other potentially hazardous machine. Think of your car, for example. Would you leave it with the keys in the ignition where a child or other irresponsible person could easily decide to "play" with it? Would you get behind the wheel when you were so tired that you couldn't concentrate or when you'd had too much to drink? Would you drive without heeding the rules of the road, drive carelessly, or speed through a heavily populated area?

Owning a firearm, like owning a car, requires maturity and responsibility. The soundest rules of firearms safety are the most commonsense.

TREAT EVERY GUN AS IF IT WERE LOADED—ALWAYS. The first rule of weapon safety is the most important. Most accidents with firearms are caused by careless handling of a loaded pistol or by carelessness when checking the chamber.

This is especially true with semiautomatics. The

cautious gun owner will not rely on the pistol's safety: He will first make sure there's no round in the chamber, and he'll carry the pistol, when he must carry it at all, with the magazine pulled out.

When you practice shooting, get in—and stay in— the habit of unloading the gun as soon as you've finished practicing. Once that habit is ingrained, you'll have less of a chance of suddenly finding yourself with a loaded gun you thought was empty.

If someone hands you his gun and assures you it's unloaded, don't take his word for it. **CONSIDER A GUN LOADED UNTIL YOU HAVE SEEN FOR YOURSELF THAT IT ISN'T. MOST IMPORTANT, MAKE SURE THE ACTION IS OPEN.** Another good rule to follow is: Treat anyone with a gun—even someone you trust more than anyone else in the world—as if that person is bound to have an accident with it. If someone hands you any shooting arm, accept it only with the muzzle pointed downward and check it immediately to make certain it isn't loaded.

By the same token, **NEVER HAND ANYONE A GUN WITHOUT FIRST POINTING THE MUZZLE END DOWN TOWARD THE GROUND WITH THE ACTION OPEN; IMMEDIATELY BEFORE HANDING OVER THE GUN, CHECK TO MAKE SURE IT ISN'T LOADED.**

Always store your handgun with the action open and no cartridges in the chamber. Always store your ammunition in a separate place, never alongside your gun. If you can store the gun and the ammunition in separate places, both of which can be locked and unlocked only by you personally, you'll be wise to do so.

Keep the muzzle of your gun pointed downward at all times, except when raising it to aim and fire. If you are resting after a shot, do so with the gun in the "rest" position, except during rapid-fire sequences.

Never attempt to use any ammunition in your handgun except that which was factory-made for the specific gun. Just because a cartridge fits it doesn't mean it can be safely used.

Before shooting, be sure of your target and what's beyond it; be sure of your backstop as well.

On the range, obey all firing-line commands immediately, and do not load your gun until ordered to.

On the range, when the command to cease firing is issued, stop immediately and unload. Then double-check to make sure the pistol is unloaded and there is no cartridge left in firing position.

Keep your finger off the trigger until prepared to shoot.

On the range, wear ear and eye protection. You'll find these required at most shooting ranges.

The best use of a handgun in a defensive situation is not to have to use one at all. The wise gun owner tries to avoid situations that may call for firearms rather than relying on the use of force for protection.

Owning a handgun doesn't make you invincible. Do all you can to avoid criminal attacks. Make your living quarters as burglarproof as possible. Take care when walking alone at night, on public transportation, and with strangers. Don't leave valuables on the seat of your car or in plain sight, whether you're in the car or not. If your car breaks down on a lonely road, get out long enough to tie a handkerchief to the antenna, then lock yourself in. Women and men who must drive alone often are well advised to invest in a CB radio.

Never open your doors to strangers, no matter the time of day. Never give your address to strangers who telephone. If you hear a noise at night, call the police instead of rushing to investigate it yourself. A great many handgun accidents occur when the pistol is used nervously or without thinking in an emergency. Don't let this happen to you.

Owning a gun can provide peace of mind and security, and for those who spend time practicing regularly at a range or with a gun club, it can mean companionship and an enjoyable pastime as well. If you own or are planning to buy a handgun, treat it with respect. Keep it well maintained, never joke around with it or treat it lightly, and never let familiarity allow you to let down your guard and grow careless.

Above all, if you own or plan to own a gun, learn to shoot it. Only by shooting it correctly can you consider ownership of a firearm a positive step in your life.